Red deer

Stuart Collier

Mike Gage

M

Macmillan Education

Acknowledgements

First published 1987

Published by
MACMILLAN EDUCATION LTD
Houndmills, Basingstoke,
Hampshire RG21 2XS
and London
Companies and representatives throughout the world

Designed by Ray Hyden, Type Generation Ltd
Illustrated by Anna Hancock

Printed in Hong Kong

British Library Cataloguing in Publication Data
Collier, Stuart
Red deer.—(Reading and language scheme. Level 2)
1. Readers—1950-
I. Title II. Gage, Mike II. Serles
428.6 PE1119
ISBN 0-333-42396-8

Red deer

The animal in this photograph is a red deer. Red deer are the largest wild animals in Great Britain, but they are very timid. Many people have never seen one of them because the deer live in lonely places that are far away from towns and cities. But we can look at photographs of deer, and then we can see how beautiful they are.

It is not easy to take photographs of deer. Like most wild animals, they usually run away if people come near. And they can run very fast.

This book is about deer and about a man who learned how to photograph them.

Who took the photographs?

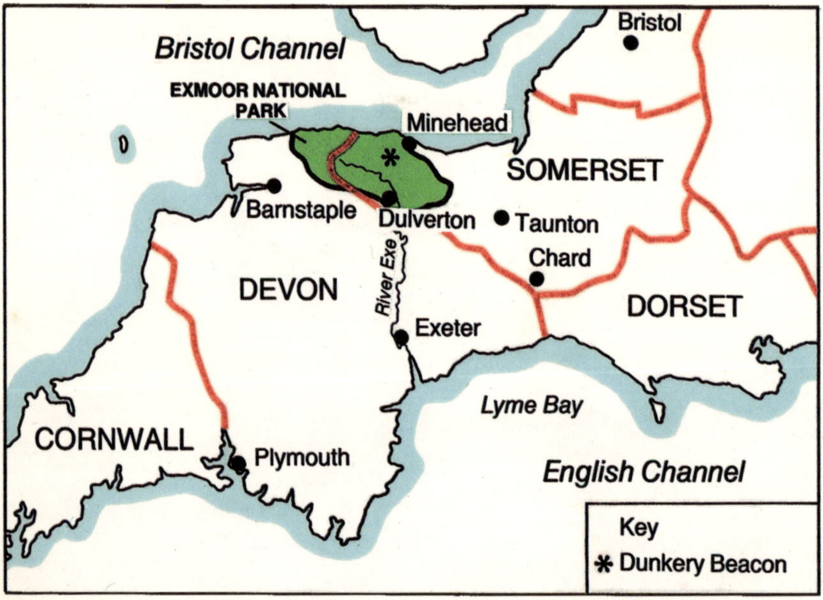

This map shows Exmoor and the place where Mike saw the deer.

The photographs in this book were taken by Mike Gage, who lives in Somerset, England. He works as a builder, but his hobby is taking photographs of the wild red deer on Exmoor, which is a large area of countryside with grass and heather and trees and bushes. This is the sort of country where deer like to live. Mike has learned how to take very good pictures of the deer, like the one on page 3. He has been interested in red deer for a long time, but he first came across them by accident. This is how it happened.

Mike lives in a small town called Chard. One morning he was driving across Exmoor on his way to work. He was going to build a wall for someone who lived in another town, called Minehead. Just as he came to a place called Dunkery Beacon, nine wild deer suddenly appeared on the road in front of him. They crossed the road and then ran off over some fields.

Quickly Mike stopped his van and got out to look. As he watched the deer running away he thought that they looked very beautiful. He wondered if he would see them again.

How Mike began his hobby

All through the day Mike kept thinking about the deer, and that evening he decided to return to Dunkery Beacon to look for them. He went back to the place where he had stopped his van in the morning and he was very lucky, for he saw the deer again. There were nine of them in the herd and they were all female deer. They were grazing a short distance away from the road, but as soon as they saw Mike they began to move away.

After this, Mike returned to Exmoor as often as he could. He read books about red deer and he began to understand their way of life. Then one day he thought that he would like to take some photographs of them. So he decided to buy himself a camera.

Mike soon discovered that it was very difficult to get good photographs of the animals. When he took pictures from a distance it was impossible to see the deer clearly because they looked so small. Whenever he tried to come near, they simply ran away. So he had to learn how to approach them without startling them.

Getting closer to the deer

Mike began to think of a way of getting very close to the wild deer. He noticed that it was often difficult to spot them when they were among trees and bushes. The colour of their coats was just like the colours of the tree-trunks and shadows, so they were very well hidden. They were **camouflaged** by their coats. So Mike decided to try to camouflage himself.

He bought some army clothes which had patches of green and brown on them, for he knew that soldiers used clothes like these when they did not want to be seen moving around in woods and fields. Before he went out, he put these clothes on. He also covered up his hands and face by wearing gloves and a long woollen cap.

When he was dressed like this, Mike found that he could get much closer to the deer. He was well camouflaged among the trees and bushes. If there were no trees, Mike lay on his stomach and crawled through the grass. But he still did not get close enough to take good photographs. The deer knew he was there even when he was invisible.

How did they know he was there?

The arrows show how the wind is blowing.
Mike is ***upwind.*** *The deer smell him and run off.*

Mike was sure that the deer could not **see** him when he was camouflaged. Then he realised that they could still **hear** him and **smell** him.

Deer have very good hearing indeed. Mike discovered that they could hear him stepping on a dead twig, or brushing against a branch, even when they were 400 metres away. He knew this because the deer lifted up their heads and twitched their ears.

Mike soon learned to stay very still when he saw them doing this. He had to wait until the deer started eating again, or they would become frightened and run away.

Now Mike often waits for twenty minutes before moving closer, if he thinks that the deer have heard him.

*Mike is **downwind**. The deer do not smell him and go on feeding.*

Deer also have a very good sense of smell. They can smell people from a long way off.

All living things have their special smell. It is called their **scent.** Mike discovered that his scent could be carried towards the deer by the wind if it was blowing against his back. This is called being **upwind** from the deer. When they smelled his scent on the wind, the deer ran off at once.

So when he is following deer, Mike always makes sure now that the wind is blowing into his face. This is called being **downwind** from the deer. When Mike is downwind, it is difficult for the deer to smell him because his scent is being carried away in the opposite direction.

Keeping a look-out

Mike noticed that a few deer always kept watch when the others were eating or sleeping. These deer are **look-outs** and they stay near the edges of the herd. They watch and listen and smell for danger. The next three photographs show what happens when a look-out deer warns the others that an enemy is approaching.

Mike has often been spotted by the look-out deer at the edges of the herd. When he is crawling towards a herd of deer, he sometimes disturbs birds like pigeons or crows. As soon as the birds fly up, the look-out deer see them. They warn the others and the herd moves away.

1. The look-out deer is standing up. The others are lying down dozing in the sun.

2. The look-out deer has warned the others of danger, so they all stand up. They are watching and listening and sniffing the air. You can see that they are worried by something.

3. Off they go! The deer all run away together.

Taking close-up pictures

As Mike learned more about following deer, he was able to get very close without frightening them. But his new hobby made him learn a lot about photography as well, and he found he could take beautiful close-up pictures from quite far away if he used a **tele-photo lens.** A tele-photo lens is like a small telescope which fits on to the front of the camera. Mike used this special lens to take most of the close-up pictures in this book.

But Mike did not need his tele-photo lens to take these two pictures of a baby deer. New-born calves keep still and hidden if their mother leaves them alone. Mike had been watching the mother and he had seen her push her calf to the ground. He had seen her going away, leaving

the calf in the ferns. So he was able to walk right up to this calf to photograph it.

The calf's mother had left it for a short while, but Mike knew that she would soon be back. He took his photographs, being very careful not to touch the calf. If a mother deer smells that someone has touched her calf, she will probably leave it to die.

Mike waited to see if he could get a picture of the mother deer and the calf together. Soon the mother came back and the calf started to suck her milk. But all at once the mother spotted Mike and started to make loud barking noises to tell him to go away. So Mike took one more picture and then left them alone.

Are all red deer wild?

Red deer are not all wild. Like cattle and sheep, some deer are kept on farms for their meat. The meat of deer is called **venison.**

Deer farms need to have very high fences. A deer could easily jump over an ordinary fence, so those on deer farms are often more than two metres high.

Sometimes Mike visits a deer farm in Devon. The picture shows him on the farm with a male deer called Rupert. You can see that Rupert enjoys having his head rubbed!

Male deer are called **stags,** and they are easy to recognise because they have horns called **antlers** on their heads. The female deer are called **hinds.** Unlike the stags, the hinds have no antlers.

How do antlers grow?

The stags grow a new set of antlers every year. Each time, the antlers get bigger, so the oldest stags have the largest antlers.

The antlers start growing in the spring, and at first they have a soft covering which is called **velvet.** During the summer they keep on growing, then in the autumn the velvet peels away and the bare horn is left underneath. The stags keep their antlers through the winter, and lose them in March and April.

Mike's photograph of antlers shows how they grow longer and more branched every year.

When do deer breed?

A stag roaring.

Stags and hinds live apart for most of the year. They have their own separate herds. But in October they come together to breed. This time is called the **rutting season.**

Stags can be dangerous in the rutting season. At that time each stag tries to gather a group of hinds around him. If he succeeds, he does not let any other stag come near. A stag may have about twelve hinds, and the most powerful ones have even more. But some stags may have none at all.

When two stags meet they roar loudly at each other. Sometimes they fight by locking their antlers together and pushing. They will sometimes also attack people who come too close. Mike has been chased by stags three times.

Once he went to the deer farm in Devon to see Rupert. It was October, and the rutting season had started. Mike was surprised when Rupert suddenly ran up behind him and started roaring loudly. Mike turned to stroke him. But instead of standing to have his head rubbed, Rupert reared up on his back legs and pawed at Mike with his front ones. Mike was not hurt but Rupert's attack taught him to be very careful of stags at this time of year.

After the rutting season is over, the stags become peaceful again. They leave the hinds and go off in search of food. Both stags and hinds must eat as much as they can before the cold winter weather comes.

A hind in the snow.

Two unusual photographs

Mike has known some of the deer since they were calves. They are now so used to seeing him that they let him come very close. They know that he will not harm them. So sometimes he has the chance to take very unusual photographs. Here are two of them.

The first one shows a white hind. White hinds are very uncommon. The usual colour of a hind's coat is dull red.

The second photograph is rather funny. This stag does not seem very happy about having his picture taken. He is sticking out his tongue at the photographer!

Mike had to practise for a long time before he could take really good photographs of the wild deer on Exmoor. He is now very skilful, but he may still spend a whole day following the deer without getting even one good picture. But at other times he has better luck. This book has shown some of the best pictures in his collection.

About the author

My name is Stuart Collier. I am a schoolteacher and I live in Somerset. I hope you have enjoyed looking at the beautiful photographs in this book. In our school, we did a project on red deer after we saw Mike Gage's pictures.

We drew and painted our own pictures of the animals. We found some old antlers and measured them and we tried to guess the ages of the stags which had lost them. We made a list of all the new words about deer that we had learned. And we wrote stories about deer and tried to imagine what it would be like to be one.

We hope that you decide to have a project too and that you enjoy doing it as much as we did.

Glossary (special words)

antlers: the horns of a stag (see stag)

camouflage: special colours on clothes, or on an animal's coat or on its skin. The colours and patterns match the things round about

camouflaged: hidden by special colours or patterns

deer calf: a baby deer

downwind: standing so that the wind carries your scent **away** from a wild animal

hind: a female deer

lens: the part of the camera that sends light on to the film. It is usually made of glass

look-out: an animal or a person who watches for an enemy

rutting season: the time in October when deer come together to breed

scent: the special smell that each living thing has

stag: a male deer

tele-photo lens: a special lens for taking close-up pictures of things that are quite far away

upwind: standing so that the wind carries your scent **towards** a wild animal

velvet: the soft covering of a stag's antlers when they are new

venison: the meat of the red deer

Index